How to Writ
of a Book on Amazon

A complete step by step guide on how to write a
review of a book on Amazon

ELIJAH RICHARD

1

Table of Contents

Chapter 1: How to Write a Book Review on Amazon

Have you actually read a book that you actually enjoyed? Did you bother to tell your friends about it? That is exactly what a book review is based on the fact that you are actually sharing your thoughts about a book.

Just like any opinion you offer, it has the advantage of not having to be accurate or incorrect. It is actually your opinion.

Please bear in mind that these tips are actually suitable for non-fiction books. Although you can actually apply them to fiction, but there are additional considerations for a review of a fiction book.

Start with who you are talking to, your audience

It is true that you speak differently to your children compared to your boss. The same goes for a book review based on the fact that you deciding who you want to tell about the book makes a difference as to what you include and how you say it.

Should in case you are thinking of what to say, then all you need do is to picture the person you are talking to as well as relating to them based on the paper work. However, in other for you to make it easier, write your review in a word processor or a text processor. Then you can just copy and paste it into the review box.

Make a decision on what to include in a book review on Amazon

1. Firstly, there is the need for you to choose the number of stars to give the book. Please do not torture yourself over this. Just choose the rating you think is appropriate.

2. Secondly, there is the need for you to have a title or headline for your review. Again, please do not spend more time on this based on the fact that it can actually be as simple as "buying this book". If you are in doubt, please do well to look at some of the reviews on other books. But please do not stress on this step.

3. Once that is done please do well to write the review. Meanwhile, one of the easiest things to include in the review is what your favorite idea or tip was. Please ensure you pick that out (you can even refer to the chapter or page) also there is the

need for you to state the reason why you liked that item.

Also, the next thing you may want to say is probably who you think would most benefit from this book. Is it for beginners? Or is it someone who is more experienced? You can easily stop your review there. Most reviews are fairly short let's say fewer than 250 words. But if you are in need of additional ideas for what you could include in your review, please do well to go through these questions:

- How does this compare to other books you've read on the topic?

- Has the information you acquired from the book been of help to you in achieve something?

- Is there a quote from the book that you can stick with?

- Has there been a change in your knowledge or opinion during the course of you reading the book?

- Was the actually author funny or entertaining?

- Where you surprise by anything?

- Are you actually looking forward to reading future books from this author?

Include negative feedback if needed

Ever since the book review is your opinion, you are actually very free to include both positive and negative comment based on the fact that they can be helpful for future readers who are considering buying this book. However, it is very important that you remember to keep the positive perspective, rather than lash out at the author.

Basically, there are some sample phrases that you can actually make use of for negative comments in your review.

- Although the book was good but, I wish the author had...

- The book would have been better if...

- I do not actually recommend this book for...

- I wish the author had included...

While you may have hesitated in writing book reviews in the past, you will discover that they have actually become easier with each one that you have written. And so the next time someone suggests that you write books review on Amazon, you will actually find it a little easier. Please do not forget that you are just sharing your opinion with your fellow readers.

How to Post a Book Review

Once you have an active Amazon account, it is actually possible for you to post your first book review. Below are the steps to follow.

1. Log in to your Amazon account.

2. Please move to the specific product page in the book that you intend to review thereafter select the book format that you want to use. Also, if you do not have a direct link to the book page, you can as well make use the search box that is at the top of the page. Please do not forget that some books have more than one edition, or are available in more than one format (such as audio book , Kindle, hardback paperback, etc.), so be ready to navigate to the page to the edition you want to review thereafter select the appropriate format.

3. Please scroll down to the Customer Reviews section and then click on the "Write a customer review" button.

4. Also in the next screen you will find the title of the book that you want to review and close to it are five light gray stars. You can also rate the book by clicking on the appropriate number of stars that you want to give the book. Your selection will however turn the stars blue. Below is a guide to the number of stars you should give.

1 = I hate it.

2 = I do not like it.

3 = its okay.

4 = I like it.

5 = I love it.

5. Also you will receive a text box below the stars. There you will write or paste in the text of your book review. After, you can also add a headline for your review, if you feel like. Please when you are done, do not forget to press the "Submit" button.

6. Again, you will receive the message saying "Thanks for your review of [the book you reviewed].

We are currently processing your review and we will email you [your email address associated with your Amazon account] as soon as this is complete."

7. Please make sure you check your email for a message from Amazon containing your book review. Also, you will see a link that contains review." well done! You have uploaded your first book review on Amazon.

How to Edit Your Book Review

Meanwhile, after you must have posted your book review, you may later decide that you want to edit or update it. However, if that be the case, below is how you can go about it.

1. Please log in to your Amazon account.

2. Please do well to proceed to the following link https://www.amazon.com/gp/cdp/member-reviews where you will see a list of all of your posted reviews.

3. Please do well to click on the "Edit review" button.

4. On the next screen you will be able to change, update or even add to your original review. This actually includes the amount of stars that you are awarded, the text of the review as well as the

headline. However, when you are done, please press the "Submit" button.

5. Once more, you will also receive a message "Thanks for your review [the book you reviewed], we are currently processing your review and we will email you [your email address associated with your Amazon account] as soon as this is completed."

6. Please check your email for a message from Amazon containing your book review. You will also see a link that contains your full review." well done! You have edited your book review on Amazon.

Chapter 2: A Book Review is NOT a Book Report

Meanwhile, I have received and seen a fair share of book reviews that could only be classified as book reports. And that is to say that these types of reviews are completely useless and as such could be annoying to other readers.

Also, many of the book report type usually include a summary of the book. Do we really need that? Generally, summary should be included in the book description. And if the summary includes too many details, then it should be labeled as "Spoiler Alert!" Also, this can impact in the sales of the book based on the fact that some potential reader buyers might feel like they have already read the book just by reading your review.

Personally, I think that these reviewers are stuck in a grade school or high school mindset, and as such, it is believed that their reviews will be judged based on whether they include details to prove that they actually read the book. Just like school-age kids, they may also think that their review will be judged based on the number of words, with more words being better (which it is not, of course).

How Long Should a Book Review Be?

Please do not forget that the buyers are looking for quick ways to assess whether to buy a book or not. It is also important to note that reviews that go on for hundreds and hundreds or even thousands of words are overwhelming. Generally, with just a few sentences or paragraphs to highlight your key assessments and opinions of the book are enough.

What Should Be Included in a Book Review?

Again, reviews that simply say "good book," or some other vague evaluation, are not helpful, even if they express positive regard for the work.

What should you write in a book review? Sometimes, even if you like a book it is usually difficult to figure out what to cover. Below are quite a few questions that could jumpstart your review as well as keeping it on track. Please note that it is not compulsory that you answer all questions based on the fact that you are only expected to pick one or a few that are relevant.

- Why did you like it (or not)?

- Was it actually too long (or short)? What length would you have preferred? What was

14

omitted and/or what should have been cut out?

- Was it simple to understand? What made it easy or difficult?

- Was it what you expected? If not, what was your expectation?

- What did you think of the author's writing style? Was it actually appropriate for this kind of book?

- Was there anything inappropriate that could turn off readers like you?

- Have this book actually change your life or perspective in anyway?

- Can you compare this book to others that you have read?

- Do you think that the book was actually worth your investment of both dollars and time?

Do you intend to break Amazon's Community Guidelines for Book Reviews?

Basically, I am actually not a fan of giving people free advance copies of the hope that they will write a review. Although, have never seen it work well, but I think it's gaming the system. Based on the fact that I also want genuine reviews for my books. But it's is actually a common practice especially in the self-publishing realm. And this practice could actually result to violation of the Amazon's Community Guidelines for reviews.

Based on that, Amazon does not permit reviews for the following when creating "content," that include book reviews:

- Products or services offered by your family, close friends, business associates, or employers.

- Anything that you have received in exchange for compensation, including "free or discounted products" or even those that you are requesting or offering compensation of any type in exchange for reviews is not permitted.

This is actually not permitted based on the fact that it is done in other to preserve the integrity of the community. Being the retail giant they are, Amazon in no doubt craves for real buyers that will review real verified purchases. And as such it is very important that you think properly before you accept any authors' or publishers' invitations for free copies of their books. But if you are an author or publisher as the case maybe, then there is also the need for you to think twice about offering these freebies in the hopes of getting reviews.

Reviewing the Reviewers

Sincerely speaking, I really do love Amazon has a system for buyers to easily vote on whether a review has been helpful or not essentially in a review of the reviewer. This is actually a good indicator if you are writing useful reviews. Take a glance at that every once in a while to see how you are doing as a book reviewer.

In case you want to see how many "helpful" votes that you have received, go to Your Account > Ordering and shopping preferences > Profile. There you will see how many reviews you have done and how many helpful votes that you have received.

In addition, in the about section of your profile, you will also see your reviewer ranking

The following are some more specific tips on how to write a book review for fiction as well as non-fiction books.

Writing a Review for Fiction Books

There are basically several things that you will want to include in your book review format .Also for a fiction book to help potential future readers all that is expected from you is for you to get information that is valuable to them.

Firstly, it important that you have a title, author, as well as genre of the book. This however will instantly narrow down the readership to only those who are interested in the idea of the book.

Thereafter, there will be the need for you to provide a brief synopsis that includes the main characters as well as a brief look into the plot.

In this section, you there is the need for you not give away anything that might ruin the book for the potential reader.

You can further move on to explain your personal impression of the book.

Also, some things that you may address would be the credibility (or lack thereof) of the characters, the names of the characters you connected to, the issues that the main characters have to face, (and why), your favorite (and least favorite) parts of the book, and if you would recommend it to other people.

Meanwhile, when giving your personal impression, make sure you are writing about the story, not about yourself.

For instance, you can state how the ending was predictable, but do not say something like, "I hate love stories."

Doing this, you will have people wondering why you read the book in the first place.

Finally, there is the need for you to mention what kind of reader that may enjoy the book.

Also for you to gain the trust of other readers there is the need for you to be honest about who may particularly like this book and those that may find it a little important.

Please note that there are a few things to keep in mind when you are doing this. Also it is important that you write a review on how the book was written, and not how you think it should have been written. Based on the fact that your opinion in this matter is not going to help other readers decide if they want to read this book.

However, it is essential that you add some of your personal thoughts into the review instead of providing people with a summary that is related to a book report.

Furthermore, there is the need for you to give your opinion about the book's quality beyond its content, and there is actually no need for you to go off on a tangent suggesting the various endings or other directions in which the book could have gone.

Chapter 3: Writing a Review for Non-Fiction Books

Writing a review for non-fiction books differs from the reviews for fiction books.

Also, you might want to start your review with background information about the author as well as the information in the book. Please it is important that you state why the author is (or is not) a trusted source of information on the subject at hand.

During the course of your write up, it is important that you let the reader know what the author's goal was while writing the book. It is also important that you bear in mind;

- The goal of the inform readers?

- To persuade them to do something?

- To teach them?

The important second step of this is for you to let the reader know if the author actually succeeded in meeting their goal. There is the need for you to provide a summary of the book as well as an evaluation of its contents. Like the strength and weaknesses, the tone and writing style of the book and its potential value for its intended audience among others.

How to Rank a book on Amazon

Meanwhile, it is possible for you to give one star of five star to a book based on how much you enjoyed it. However, it is important that you think properly before giving either a one star or a five star as the case maybe.

Five-star reviews are basically books that are left for great writing, great editing, and an impactful storyline that makes you want to read it several times.

Although , most times the wise thing to do is to give five stars to every book that you think is pretty good, but it does not help potential readers to know if this book is worth their time.

Again, when a book is written and edited well, you should not give it fewer than three stars.

You can also provide explanation in your review telling readers why you did not like a book, but if on the other hand it is well written and you give it one or two stars, you are making your review too subjective.

Also, there is the need for you to permit other readers the chance to make their own decision on the content of the book based on the fact that others may find the content to be great.

Again, unless a book has absolutely no redeeming qualities at all and the writing has errors and typos, only on that ground can you not give a one-star review. As a self-published author, t is important that you know that poor reviews can be are very distressing to authors, especially if they stand no ground.

In addition, getting a negative review from a fellow author can be even more painful compared to when a reader is reading and passing it.

Basically, authors often focus on the negative points in reviews, even if they are mainly positive, and as such there is the need for you to be careful to tread lightly.

Also, knowing the potential lasting effect that a negative review can have on an author's reputation and personal feelings can show you the importance of leaving thoughtful reviews.

What this do not mean actually is that you have to be gentle in your criticism, as well as been careful in the delivery of your opinions.

It is important to note that every book may have something about it that you do not like.

And as such, there is the need for you to lighten up your book critique as well as finding some ways to put a positive spin on your comments.

For example, In case you happen to read a book on a subject and it is geared more on beginners but does not suggest that in the book's title, I would suggest you say that; "The book is a great tool for those who want to brush up, only on the basics."

And that means that you can be critical without being harsh.

In conclusion, the trick in writing an effective book review is to approach the task in a systematic way.

Also, there is the need for you to focus on the main points that you want to communicate to future readers as well as think about what readers want to get out of your review.

Again, the book reviews should communicate the quality as well as the style of the book with no much detail that will make the readers not to read the book further in other to gain more information.

However, what I would suggest is that if you genuinely do not like the book, please do not start with a diatribe about its awfulness, like;

- This book is so bad I would not use it to line the kitty litter tray.

- Also please try to give specific reasons.

- The plot was full of holes/ the characters were clichéd/ the pace was too slow and I lost interest.

Or all of the above.

In that case, it means that you are giving other readers an indication of why they might or might not like the book.

In case you don't know it is one the useful feedback that the author needs. Also, no one can deny that negative reviews hurt (any author who does is lying) and if it is just the occasional one, you read it and can as well try to forget it.

Again, if you are getting a ton of reviews that say that your plot drags or your characters are dull, then there is the need for you to give serious consideration to the fact they could be right. However, there is one proviso to this and that is;

Do not read a book in a genre that you are not a fan of and then post a review saying how much you hated it.

You can however end up by just end up showing your lack of knowledge as in:

The Billionaire's Marriage Tryst is lame. There is actually too much emphasis on unrequited love along with Arabella and Brandon end up in each other's arms at the end and that was so predictable.

Or you can as well say that Vampires on Mars is a crap book based on the fact that it was such a weird concept, full of way out creatures and places, and things that could not possibly happen in real life.

Chapter 4: Screenshots from Amazon on how to write a book review

Method 1 of 2:

Using Amazon.com on a Computer

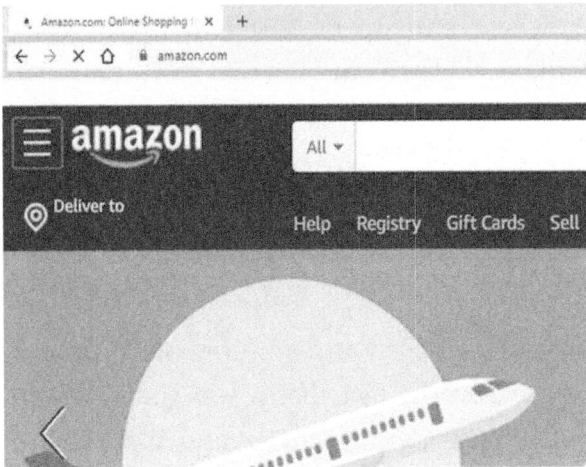

1. **Please go to** https://www.amazon.com. As soon as you have spent adequate time with your product you can leave a helpful review, by opening Amazon's website in any of your preferred web browser.

- In case you need tips on writing helpful and objective Amazon reviews, check out How to Write an Objective Amazon Review.

- Please the customer reviews must meet Amazon's Community Guidelines, which you can find here: https://www.amazon.com/gp/help/customer/display.html?nodeId=201929730

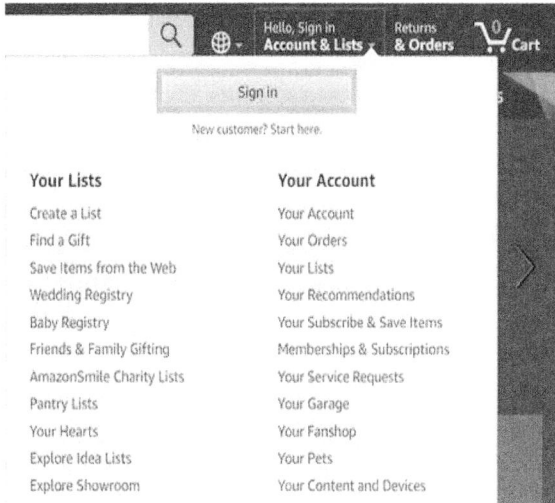

2. **Please sign in to your account.** In case you see the option to sign in near the top-right corner of the page (above "Accounts & Lists"), please click Sign in to do so now. Also, if you see your name there it means that you have already signed in.

- More so, if can no longer access the Amazon account that you used to purchase the product, you can as well leave a review using a different account. But it won't be marked with the "Verified Purchase" badge. You can also review the product by searching for it on Amazon as well as clicking on Write a Customer Review on the left side of the review section.

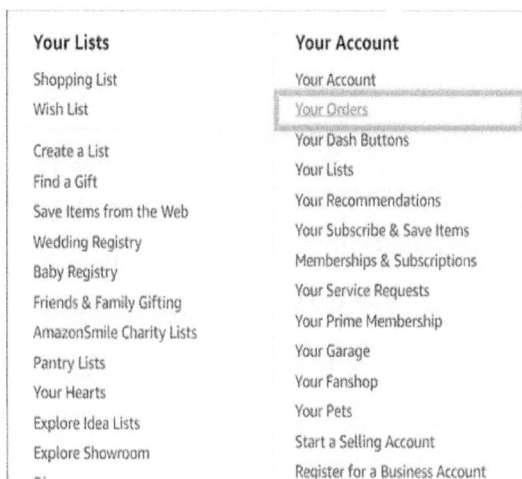

Your Lists	Your Account
Shopping List	Your Account
Wish List	Your Orders
Create a List	Your Dash Buttons
Find a Gift	Your Lists
Save Items from the Web	Your Recommendations
Wedding Registry	Your Subscribe & Save Items
Baby Registry	Memberships & Subscriptions
Friends & Family Gifting	Your Service Requests
AmazonSmile Charity Lists	Your Prime Membership
Pantry Lists	Your Garage
Your Hearts	Your Fanshop
Explore Idea Lists	Your Pets
Explore Showroom	Start a Selling Account
	Register for a Business Account

3. **Please ensure that you click the Orders menu**. It' is actually close to the top-right corner of the page next to "Accounts & Lists." This will actually takes you to a page that displays your recent Amazon orders. Meanwhile, it is best that you review an item directly from your orders rather than just search for the product on Amazon's website.

This will actually ensures that you are reviewing the correct version or edition of the product.

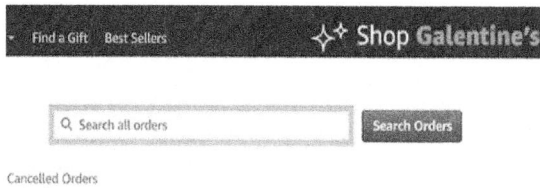

4. **Please locate the order containing the product that you want to review.** Here if you ordered for an item within the past six months, you can actually locate the order by scrolling down the current page. But if the item was purchased prior to that time, please click the drop-down menu that says past six months (above the first order) thereafter select a different time period.

- Also, you can search for the item by typing its name into the "Search all orders" blank and then click on Search Orders.

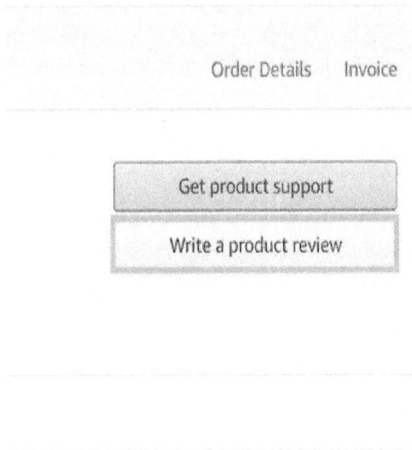

Order Details   Invoice

Get product support

Write a product review

5. **Please click Write a product review next to the order**. The button is actually and it is at the right of the order's contents. Please if there is only one item in the order, opens a page that allows you to review just that item.

- Again, if the order contains two or more items, please clicking this link will display thumbnails of all ordered items, with the selected order's items appearing at the top of the page.

- Also, if you do not see the option to click Write a product review, and thereafter click on order details to expand the contents of the order and click the product's title to view its page. You can also scroll down and then click to write a customer review to the left of the first existing customer review.

☆☆☆☆☆

Why did you like or dislike this product?

6. **Please select an overall star rating**. More so, you can rate an item from one to five stars. And so, if you want to rate one star (the lowest rating), please click the first star. To rate 5 stars, please click on the fifth star.

- Also, if you have selected an order that contained one or more item. Please note that selecting your start rating will open the remaining parts of the review screen for that item.

- Again, if you ordered a functional item, such as earplugs, you may now see the opportunity to select a star rating for the product's usefulness and other details.

Headline for your review

⊙ Add a photo

Submit

7. **Please do not forget to add a photo or video (optional) of the product.** Should in case you took a photograph or video of the item you are reviewing (optional), please

click the + under "Add a photo or video" to upload it from your computer.

8. **Please type your review**. In this part, the box at the bottom of the review form is where you can be specific about what you liked or disliked about the item. Meanwhile, you can also add a title to your review (e.g., "Buy this book!").

9. **Please click on Submit**. This is actually the yellow button below the form's bottom-right corner. As soon as your review passes a quick quality review process, it will be posted to the product's page.

- Although it t may take up to 48 hours for the review to get approved but if it doesn't get approved after about three days, you can email review-appeals@amazon.com for assistance.

Method 2 of 2:

Using the Mobile App

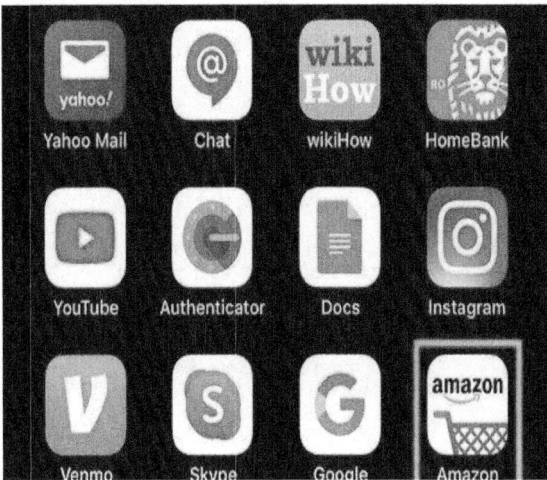

1. Please open the Amazon app on your phone or tablet. It is actually the shopping cart icon that is labeled "Amazon." However, you can easily locate it on the home screen, in the app drawer, or by searching.

- In case you are in need of tips on writing helpful and objective Amazon reviews, please do well to check out How to Write an Objective Amazon Review.

- Please in the customer reviews, the review must meet Amazon's Community Guidelines, which you can find here: https://www.amazon.com/gp/help/customer/display.html?nodeId=201929730

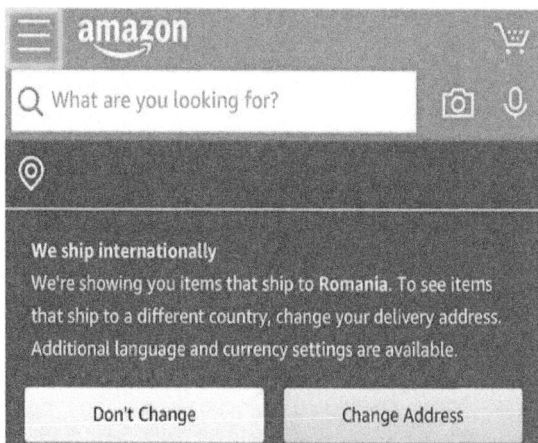

2. **Tap the ≡menu**. This is actually at the top-left corner of the screen.

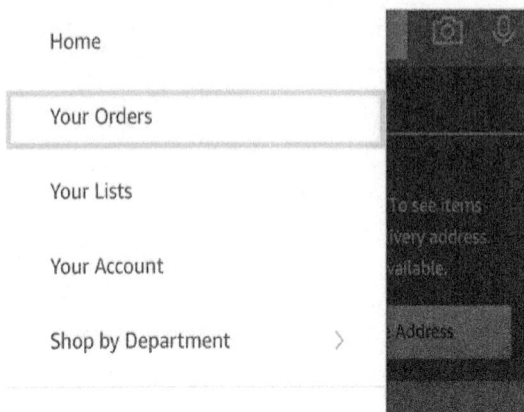

3. **Please do not forget to tap Your Orders**. It is actually located toward the top of the menu.

- Should in case you are no longer able to access the Amazon account that you used to purchase the product, you can still leave a review with a different account. But it won't be marked with the "Verified Purchase" badge. Also, if you want to review the product, please go to its page on Amazon and click write a Customer Review to the left of the review list.

Buy it again	>
Get product support	>
Write a product review	>
View order details	>

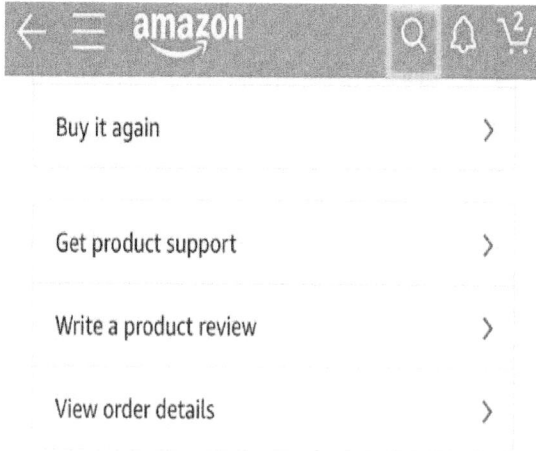

4. **Please locate the order containing the product you want to review.** Here, if you ordered an item within the past six months, you can actually find the order by scrolling down the current page.

- Also, if the item was purchased prior to that time, please do well to tap the Filter orders menu near the top-right corner of the order list, thereafter select a different time period, and then tap Apply.

- It is also very possible for you to search for the item by tapping Search all orders near the top-right corner, typing the product name, and then tapping the Search or Enter key.

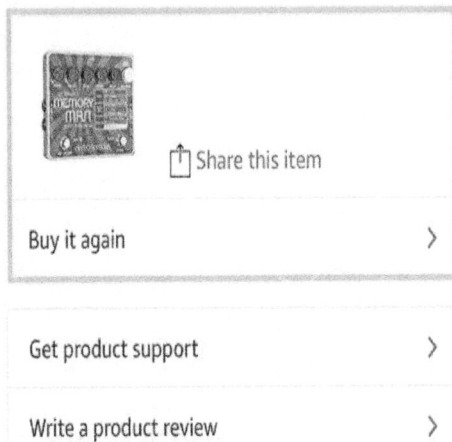

5. **Please do not forget to tap the item you want to review**. This actually opens the item's options on a separate page.

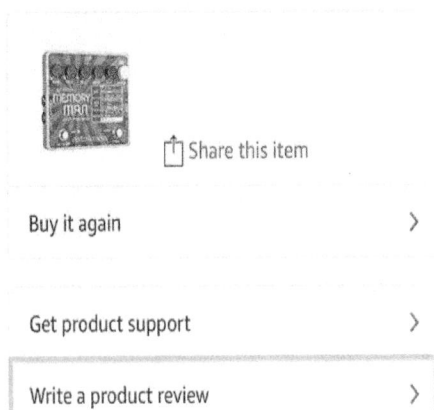

6. **Please do well to tap Write a product review.** This is actually located under the "How's your item?"

| |
| |

| Headline for your review |

| ⓞ Add a photo |

| Submit |

7. **Please ensure to tap Photo/Video to attach a photo or video of the item (optional).** Here, if you captured a photo or video of the item that you want to include with your review, this option will actually permit you to upload it now.

☆☆☆☆☆

Why did you like or dislike this product?

8. **Please select an overall star rating**. Here, you can rate an item from one to five stars. In case you want to rate one star (the lowest rating), please tap the first star but if it is five stars that you have decided to rate, please tap the fifth star.

- Again, if you have ordered a functional item, such as headphones or a lamp, there is actually the opportunity for you to select star ratings for the product's usefulness, comfort, as well as other details.

☆☆☆☆☆

> Why did you like or dislike this product?

9. **Please enter the details of your review.**
   Here, the first typing area in the "Write your
   review" section provides you the opportunity
   to describe your experience with the product.
   Please do well to enter at least seventy five
   characters that you think will be of help to
   other shoppers that will decide whether to
   purchase or skip this product.

Headline for your review

⊙ Add a photo

Submit

10. **Please enter a headline**. In this aspect, to include a title with your review, there is the need for you to tap the "Add a headline" box and type something catchy or helpful that encourages shoppers to read your review.

Headline for your review

⊙ Add a photo

Submit

11. **Please make sure you tap the yellow Submit button.** This is actually at the bottom of the review area. As soon as your review passes a short quality review process, it will be added to the product's page.

- Meanwhile, it may take up to 48 hours for the review to get approved. But if it doesn't get approved after about three days, you can email review-appeals@amazon.com for assistance

Printed in Great Britain
by Amazon